Caroline and Us

Caroline and Us

M E Davies

ATHENA PRESS
LONDON

Caroline and Us
Copyright © M E Davies 2007

All Rights Reserved

No part of this book may be reproduced in any form
by photocopying or by any electronic or mechanical means,
including information storage or retrieval systems,
without permission in writing from both the copyright
owner and the publisher of this book.

ISBN 10-digit: 1 84748 045 4
ISBN 13-digit: 978 1 84748 045 3

First Published 2007 by
ATHENA PRESS
Queen's House, 2 Holly Road
Twickenham TW1 4EG
United Kingdom

Printed for Athena Press

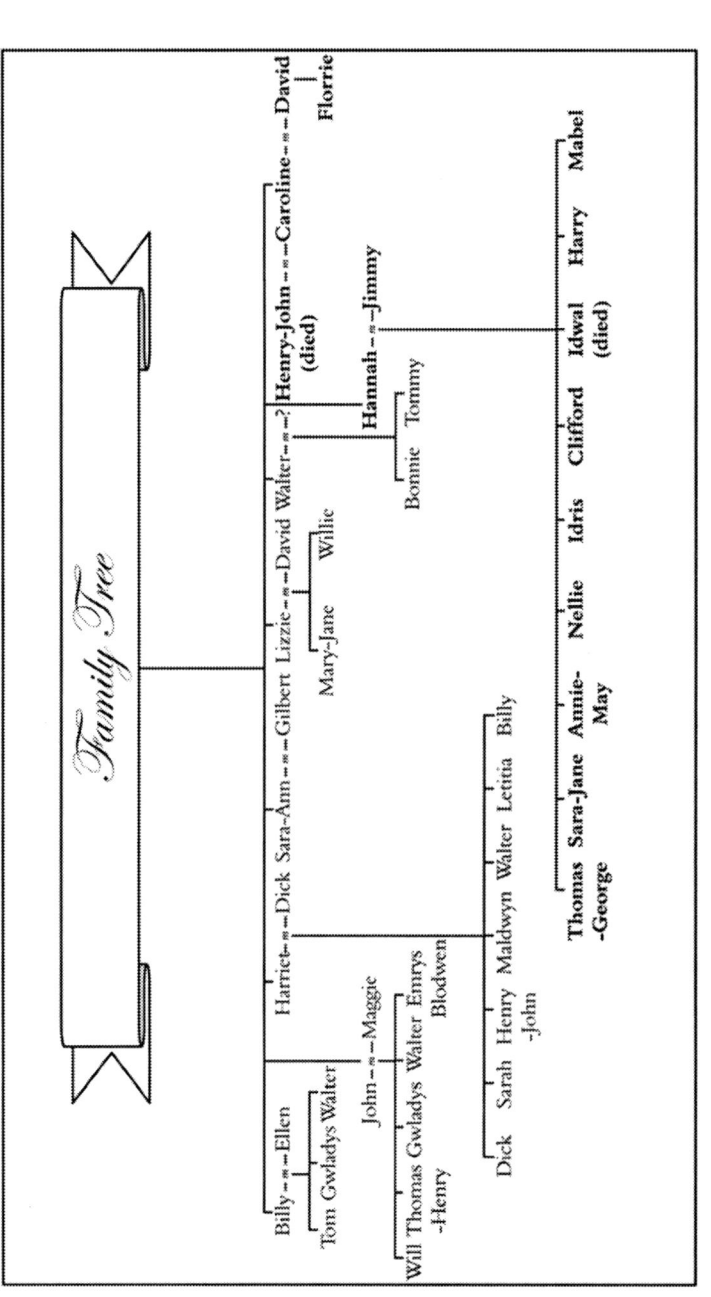

Contents

The Black Dog	9
Fresh Start	21
Outbreak of War	25
Times of Change	32
Hard Times	39
London	42
Loss and Love	52
War is Declared	58
Health Worries	69
Looking Back	78

The Black Dog

IT WAS there. It was definitely there. Caroline had seen this big black dog at the foot of the stairs, but now it was nowhere to be found. She asked her husband, Henry-John, whether he had let a black dog out of the house; but he said that he had not even seen one. A shiver ran through her. She felt that this was a bad omen, regardless of whether it had been a real dog or not.

Henry-John was a 'fireman' down the mine. It was his job to lay and set off the dynamite in the seam to loosen the coal and make more available for the men to work. She begged him to stay at home that day; she had such a bad feeling about the black dog. He laughed off her fears and told her that it was probably a trick of the light, but she knew differently. It was his day to do the firing, and if he did not go down to the mine, the men would lose a day's work. And so, reluctantly, she filled his food box and his flask of tea. She tried once more to persuade him to stay at home, but to no avail.

She tried to carry on as normally as possible. She fetched young Clifford from his bed, washed him, dressed him and fed him, but her mind was not on what she was doing. She was listening for the hooter which signalled an accident down the mine. Clifford was her sister Hannah's son. He loved staying with them as Henry-John would play with him and could be very amusing. Caroline – who her family knew as Carrie – often relieved her sister of Clifford as Hannah was pregnant again.

She took Clifford back to his mother after she had finished her work. She was glad to get out of the house. She had never been happy there as she'd always felt that it was an unlucky house for them. Henry-John had had several accidents since they had been living there; he'd had none before that.

Hannah's house was nearer to the mine in Abernant than hers. She could get there quicker than she could from home when the alarm was sounded. She did not doubt that it would sound; she was so sure that the black dog had been a warning.

She busied herself making tea for Hannah and herself before the children came home from school. Hannah was sorting out clothes for the new baby and she certainly was not short of them; although she was barely thirty-three years of age, this would be her eighth child. Thomas-George, her firstborn, had already started work and the few shillings he was able to give her each week were indeed a blessing as her husband was a poor provider. He was a nice enough man and a good worker, when he wasn't drunk – which was not very often. Sara-Jane had just finished her apprenticeship as a tailoress. Annie-May, who had inherited Hannah's beautiful auburn hair, was quite a flirt; so Hannah hoped she would marry young so that her husband would keep her under control. Nellie and Idris were still at school and Clifford was looking forward to joining them before the new baby was born. Hannah had had another boy called Idwal, but he had died when he was nine months old; he would have been the youngest.

Hannah tried to keep Caroline's mind occupied by asking her opinion about the baby clothes. They were all beautifully made by Hannah who was a qualified tailoress and so made all the clothes for her children herself. She had nearly succeeded in taking Caroline's mind off her fears when the dreaded alarm sounded. The colour drained away from Caroline's face; for a moment or two she was unable to rise from her chair. Although she had been expecting it, it was still a shock.

Caroline soon joined the throng of women moving like a torrent down Commercial Street. Some were running while others were held back by the infants in their arms or the toddlers at their sides. These were the women with no families to relieve them of the children. Caroline, like many others, walked with leaden feet, dreading the horrors that lay before them. As they approached the pit, some lucky women were already coming away, helping to support their menfolk who had survived physically but with the horror of their experience still etched on their faces. In spite of all that was going on down the mine, there seemed to be a hush over the place – that was until they started bringing out the wounded. Then the familiar wailing began, as the women saw the extent of some of the injuries. This was not a new experience for these women; it was happening far too frequently. Caroline stood alone, fearing the worst. She was not wrong. One of the officials came up to her and told her that Henry-John's body had been recovered. But they refused to let her see him as he was so badly injured. She did not argue; she just turned on her heel and walked back, in her own personal nightmare, to Hannah. Hannah took her in her arms and only then did the tears come.

★

Caroline and Us

Their sister, Lizzie, had heard the bad news and had come to Hannah's to try and comfort Caroline as best she could. When she had exhausted herself crying, they managed to persuade her to go to bed in the girls' bedroom. Lizzie said that Hannah's girls could sleep at her place. Hannah's house had one big living room behind which there was a small bedroom where the girls slept, and a small scullery.

Lizzie lived next door in the garden house. At that time it was a beautiful garden with rose arches across the path. Lizzie was one of the twins; Sara-Ann was the other one and lived in Nant-y-Moel. Lizzie had a son and daughter and was married to David who was a little too fond of his beer. Sara-Ann was married to Gilbert who was a good husband; they had no children. Caroline and Hannah, being the two youngest daughters of a large family, were very close, their mother having died suddenly at the age of fifty-six.

Their two elder sisters were also married and had large families. Maggie and her husband, John, lived in Grovesend with their family of three boys and a girl, with another child due to arrive at any moment; Harriet's first husband had died, but after a respectable period of time she had married his brother. Between these two sisters, there were three boys and three girls. Caroline's eldest brother, Billy, lived in Ferndale with his neat little wife Ellen. They had one daughter and two sons.

The idol of Caroline's family was the youngest son, Walter. I do not know why, because the only one he ever wrote to was Billy. Perhaps distance lent enchantment, as he had emigrated to America.

Henry-John

Caroline and Henry-John

Sara-Ann and Gilbert

Ellen, Gwladys and Tom

Normally, it did not take Caroline long to clean her little house and prepare the dinner, so she was able to spend much of her time with Hannah, who always seemed to be sewing. She made white sailor suits for the younger children in summer, and navy ones for the winter. The older girls would describe the fashion trend they wished to follow and she would make something to suit. Sometimes Caroline and Hannah would spend most of the afternoon making toast for the family. It had to be made in front of an open fire, and they had to change places periodically because their faces were also getting toasted.

They would chat away and Hannah would tell her all the funny stories involving the children. She told her one time about Lizzie back when her children were younger. Lizzie had come rushing in one morning in quite an agitated state. She was laughing one minute and crying the next. Hannah said she had given her a cup of tea and calmed her down, then instructed her to sit and tell her what had happened. Lizzie had left Mary-Jane sitting in her high chair, and Willie, who was five, was seated at the table drawing and had gone upstairs to make the beds. She could hear the children chattering away so she thought that everything was fine. When she came downstairs, however, Mary-Jane was holding something up to her eye. She rushed to the child and took it away from her. Her husband, David, was an underground fireman and not a very careful one at that. Willie had given Mary-Jane a stick of dynamite to use as a telescope to see the pretty pictures in the fire! They could all so easily have been blown up and Lizzie could not get this thought out of her mind. I imagine David's meal that day was a good portion of 'tongue pie'.

Caroline and Us

★

Caroline had so exhausted herself crying that, mercifully, she slept right through until early the next morning. She knew that Hannah would be up because she had to stir the fire into life in order to warm the room and to make the children's breakfast. Fire was her only means of cooking; there were no such things as gas stoves in those days. The crying was over, but the grief in Caroline's eyes when she asked what she was going to do without Henry-John nearly broke Hannah's heart. She quietly told her sister that she would cope, as she had always done. Thomas-George offered to go to the undertaker's on his way to work, but Caroline said that as Mr Zachariah only lived at the end of her road she would call in herself. Hannah wanted her to stay with her, but Caroline insisted on going home. She said that the longer she left it, the harder it would be. It was arranged that Annie-May would stay at her house and that Clifford would go home with her to give her some sense of normality. Caroline and Henry-John used to have such good times together, but particularly when looking after Clifford. They'd had five happy years of marriage and now she was a widow at the age of twenty-five.

Henry-John had no relatives apart from a distant cousin who lived near the mine in Abernant, so all the arrangements for the funeral were left to Caroline. Thomas-George was too young to be of help, and Jimmy, Hannah's husband, was so sodden with drink that he hardly knew which day of the week it was. Mr Zachariah brought Henry-John's body home to rest until the funeral as there were no chapels of rest in those days. He had done a good job of tidying up the body; apart

Caroline and Us

from a large wound on Henry-John's scalp, which must have been the cause of death. He had enclosed Henry-John's shattered body in a shroud. Had Caroline wanted her husband to be buried in his best suit, Mr Zachariah would have been faced with an almost impossible task. Caroline's house, like Hannah's, had a large living room and a very small room downstairs. Caroline's little room ran alongside her living room, and it was in that little room that the coffin was placed. She was grateful to Lizzie for bringing her some flowers to put in the room: that was all she could do for Henry-John now. She was relieved when the funeral was over as it meant that she could now grieve in her own time. In the time before the funeral the house had never seemed to be empty, as people had come to offer their sympathy.

She had been very wise to take Clifford home with her as there were days when she felt that she had nothing to get out of bed for; and there she would have stayed, sinking deeper into depression, had she not had the boy to look after. She had not been to Hannah's for over a week, which was unusual, but Hannah thought it best to let her sister do her grieving. She knew that Caroline was all right, as Annie-May slept in her house every night and reported back to her. One Sunday morning, Hannah sent Thomas-George to fetch Caroline and told him that he must not come home without her. He did not have to do much persuading, as Caroline, being a sensible woman, had decided she had to get on with her life. She knew that she would have to find employment, as all she had to live on were her savings. Henry-John had earned a reasonable wage as he was paid for doing a dangerous job. Caroline had been able to save a fair amount.

Life soon became as normal as possible, with Caroline

spending her time helping Hannah, who pretended to be far more helpless than she really was. Harry was born in May and it was then that Caroline decided it was time to make a move. Henry-John had died just before Christmas, so she had been living on her savings since then. She had received one hundred pounds in compensation, but she could not bring herself to spend any of it yet, as it did not feel right that she should benefit from his death.

She told Hannah that she intended to apply for a post as house mother at the cottage homes in Llwydcoed. The post was residential, so she would finally be able to give up the house that she hated so much. As was the custom, she visited the local councillors to ask for their support, as they would be responsible for making the appointment. She had no doubt that she was capable of the work and the interviewing panel must have agreed, as she had the good fortune to be appointed. She had two weeks to sort out her home before she started work so Hannah took whatever she needed from the house, and the remainder was sent to the auction rooms. When Caroline closed the door of that house for the last time, she felt as if a burden had been lifted off her shoulders. She would be able to forget the black dog, although it was some years before she could look at a black dog without shuddering.

Fresh Start

It was a glorious day when the sisters boarded the tram to go to Llwydcoed, which was about three miles from Aberdare. May (being a modern miss, she had decided to drop the Annie, like her great friend and cousin Mary-Jane, who became just Mary) was looking after the children so that their mother could go with Caroline to help her with her personal belongings, and give her some moral support as she started her new life.

Caroline knew that she was going to be happy working in the homes; she had already met the other 'mothers'. There were four identical houses and a larger one for the master and matron. Each house had about eight or more children; two of them were older girls who helped with the little ones. The children called their carer 'mother'. The mother did her own cleaning and had no other help, but the houses were gleaming and well appointed and they were very happy places, full of love and something which seems to be missing today – respect.

Although the children loved their parents and enjoyed their visits, there were no tears when they left; they knew where they were best looked after. They had all the care and attention they needed, weekly pocket money and a huge well-equipped playing field. The one thing that was not so good was the fact that they wore a uniform so everyone knew where they came from; the teenagers amongst them found it demeaning.

Caroline and Us

Caroline soon settled in, as she had only a few of her personal belongings with her. There was quite a walk from where the tram stopped in Trecynon to the homes in Llwydcoed, so she could only bring a few things at a time. She had brought with her the only mementos she had kept of Henry-John: his photograph and his much-loved and much-used cigarette holder. This was rather unusual as it was made in the shape of a small pipe decorated with carvings. It was kept in a leather case which showed signs of wear (I still have the pipe in its case).

Caroline with the other mothers (Miss Harris has the lace collar)

She found that dealing with the children came easily to her, as she was so used to Hannah's children. She became friendly with Miss Harris, the mother of the adjacent cottage home, and this friendship was a long and happy one. She also made a friend in Miss Baker, who had no connections with the homes but lived opposite. Miss Baker was an expert at making wine, and one day they had a great deal of fun because of it. David Eynon was an agent for Singer sewing machines and Thomas-George was being trained by him. They called on Miss Baker one afternoon and she gave them a glass of parsnip wine. It was so potent that when they went out into the open air they were reeling about as if they were drunk (which they probably were). They were forced to sit on the bank at the side of the road for over an hour before they could go on their way.

David Eynon had met Caroline several times in Hannah's house and had taken quite a fancy to her, but she was not in the least bit interested in him or in getting married again, for that matter. David, however, was not that easily put off. He, too, had been widowed; his wife had died when their baby daughter was only six weeks old. Hannah liked him very much and thought he would make a good husband for Caroline so she encouraged him; finally Caroline weakened and agreed to go out with him.

Caroline in her Sunday best

Outbreak of War

LIFE now began to get rather hectic as there were three weddings within a short space of time. This was probably because war had been declared and the couples wanted to marry before the men were called up. Sara-Jane married Jared, Mary married Ted, and May married Jack. All three girls had very good husbands; so different from their own fathers. Jack was the only one not to go into the army as he failed his medical.

Hannah had a haunted look about her for some time, as she was dreading the day that Thomas-George would have to enlist. When the dreaded call-up papers arrived at last, Hannah wept for days. She could not bear to go to the station to see him off – he was her first boy and had a special place in her heart.

After she'd had a good weep, she dried her tears and got on with her life. She had no time to mope as she had the other children to care for. Her main problem was Idris – a lovable scamp who was always up to mischief. Hannah's husband, Jimmy, could not discipline the boy as Idris had no respect for him. He adored his mother and would run errands for people and go down the station to carry suitcases, bringing every penny he earned back to Hannah.

You could say that 1916 was a productive year for the family. Sara-Jane had a daughter in January and she named her Caroline after her aunt, and Hannah had another daughter in March (me!). She wrote to let

Thomas-George know that I had arrived and he asked her to name me after his fiancée, Mabel. I never liked the name and, to add insult to injury, he never married her. She could not wait for him and married someone else. I was also given a second name suggested by David Eynon. On his rounds he had heard a woman calling her daughter Eirwen and he thought it was a pretty name; and so I was called Mabel Eirwen. Six weeks later, May produced a son and she named him Leslie. Mary was not going to be left out, so in October Phyllis arrived.

Caroline and David had a quiet wedding. I know her wedding dress was dove grey because in later years, when I had been particularly good, I was allowed to dress up in it. By the time they married, Caroline had stopped working at the homes in Llwydcoed. Business had been good for Singer throughout the war and they asked David to open a shop for them. He and Caroline found a suitable premises on Gadlys Road. It was a double-fronted shop, but the living quarters needed a good deal of alterations – it was now that Caroline felt she could use her compensation money. She put it towards the purchase and cost of alterations to the property; it became quite a modern house. There was a bathroom and toilet upstairs, as well as an outside toilet attached to the house. They had a large front bedroom – actually two rooms knocked into one – and there were two more average-sized bedrooms. The bedrooms were needed as they had Florrie, David's daughter, and Clifford, who had remained living with Caroline.

Caroline was concerned about Hannah as she'd had a difficult pregnancy and had to go to the hospital in Cardiff for the birth. Her health was deteriorating and she was beginning to look quite gaunt; she had been able to feed her other babies herself, but was too weak to feed me. When I was five months old, Hannah died from cancer of the colon. The whole family were grief-stricken, but it was Caroline and Idris who felt her loss the most. Caroline had no hesitation about taking me home with her. Uncle Billy, being the eldest member of the family, felt it was his duty to offer me a home so Auntie Ellen came over from Ferndale to fetch me. Caroline took me for a very long walk that day, which did not end until Ellen boarded the bus back to Ferndale – she had made up her mind that I was hers. There was no friction over it as Uncle Billy's conscience was clear; he had made the offer.

People would say to Caroline, 'Is that your poor sister's child? You'll never rear her.' I had the pale skin that often goes with auburn hair, which made me look delicate, but they had not counted on Caroline's determination and willpower. When she undertook to do something, she never gave up. She certainly never gave up on me although I had most of the childhood illnesses before I was able to start school, gone six years of age, and I am still here at eighty-four. David and Caroline became my mother and father.

When I was eighteen months old, we had a tragedy in the family. Idris was devastated after the death of his mother, and took to spending every Sunday afternoon with his aunt Lizzie. One Sunday, Lizzie had a special meeting at the chapel so he was at a loose end. He joined up with some friends and they went to the Cwm for a walk. This was a little valley at the base of the mountain. There was a pig farm which was surrounded by high walls so that they could not see the pigs. His friends dared him to climb an electric pylon so that he could see the pigs. Never one to refuse a dare, he did so, and was electrocuted.

Apparently Idris had been very fond of me. He used to take me to the market and when he brought me home I would have handfuls of sweets; on one occasion I came home draped in bead necklaces! My mother hoped that he had paid for them, but with Idris you never could tell. He and May were very much alike: full of life and full of mischief. May and I had the same colour hair, and one day she sent me home with a plait of her hair hanging from my head. It was the time when women were having their hair cut for the first time. When my mother had hers cut, she went around all day with her hat on for fear of what my father would say. My father and mother were not keen on Clifford visiting May on a Sunday because they played cards and that simply was not done then. We were not even allowed to sew or knit on a Sunday.

I seemed to have been nothing but trouble to my parents when I was little. When I was about five, my mother was running a fish and chip shop near the park. I was told to get myself ready as we were going over to the shop to visit her. In those days we wore leather gaiters that buttoned up the side of the leg. I knelt on a chair to reach the buttonhook that was hanging on the wall when I felt a terrible pain – whoever had made the gaiter had left a needle in the lining and it had gone straight into my knee! The doctor thought that he had removed the whole of the needle, but I was still in agony, so my mother insisted that I had an X-ray, which was something quite new then. Sure enough, there was still a piece of the needle in my knee. It prevented me from walking for quite some time and the doctor said that I was lucky not to have been crippled.

Caroline with Mabel as a baby

Mabel at eighteen months

We had a very happy home life on the whole. We did a great deal of socialising as my father loved company. Harry used to come and stay with us very often when life became difficult at home with his father. Nellie, who was now in her teens, kept house for them – not an enviable task. Harry came to us full-time eventually as Nellie had met Andy and wanted to get married. The only problems were caused by Florrie who had developed what might be called a personality disorder. She would go to her relatives and the neighbours, telling them untrue stories of what was happening at home, in order to gain their sympathy. She would put on a hangdog expression which quite spoilt her appearance as she was fairly pretty otherwise, with beautiful skin and hair. I know she loved us and we never quarrelled but she also resented us. This was quite understandable as she had been her father's only companion after her grandmother had died. She was ten years old when he married Caroline and now she had to share his love with all of us.

As a toddler I would stand at the back of my father's chair combing his hair for ages. He loved it and so did I as he had a beautiful silver quiff at the front of his head. His hair had turned grey at the age of twenty-seven when he had rheumatic fever. The illness also left him with a heart murmur – this being the reason he failed his medical for the army. He had to work in a coal mine instead, but often said he would have preferred to be in the trenches. Luckily for him he was well-educated and intelligent and was put to work in the offices of the mine, although he was not there for long as the war ended soon after.

Times of Change

THOMAS-GEORGE had now come home from the war. He had spent many months in hospital in Mesopotamia, as it was then called. A bullet had shattered his elbow and gone across his back but fortunately he was left only slightly disabled. Some things always remain in your mind. I remember that he brought me a little toy lamb on a green stand which I could pull along, and he and his friend seemed to win an endless supply of coconuts at the fair.

When my mother was not busy, she and I would sit by the fire and she would teach me little songs and rhymes which she had learned as a child. She also told me tales about the family – this is how I know about the black dog. The miners were given extra money called 'Sankey's Award', named after the man who got the money from the owners of the mines on behalf of the underpaid workers. Singer were so busy because of this that they wanted to open a shop in the town. My father introduced his brother-in-law to the company and he was given the shop. We were even able to afford to go on holiday which most people could not do back then. However, my mother had to give up her shop as she had trouble with her eyes and had to wear dark glasses for almost a year. The doctor said that it was neuritis, probably caused by the cooking fumes.

The good times came to an end and Singer had to close one of the shops, so they decided to keep the one in the town. We then opened our shop selling confectionery and dry goods and my father hoped that Florrie would take an interest in it, but she did not. She was intelligent and he hoped that she would carry on with her education but she refused – she was adamant that she wanted to go into service. My father was a proud man and this is not what he wanted for his daughter but through the Christian Delphian Church, of which my father was a member, a post was found for her in Maerdy. She was only there a fortnight before she begged my father to fetch her home. Once again through the Church she was found a job in Lonsdale House, Clapham; it was a home for disabled soldiers. She settled down very happily and members of the Church looked after her and made her welcome in their homes. My mother and I spent a very enjoyable week with her in London and met some of her friends, although not long after, my father was warned that she was getting too fond of one of the soldiers so he fetched her home. It was a pity because she was happy there, but she was young and impressionable and he did not want her to do something that she might regret later. She then went to work as Miss Templeton's maid in the Merthyr Infirmary.

It was quite a pleasant place to work in, and Phyllis and I used to love visiting her there. (Phyllis was, in fact, my second-cousin but was about the same age as me.) However, there always seemed to be dramas when Florrie came home; there would be floods of tears over her feet or her legs or because Miss Templeton had been unkind. My mother understood her problem but she would let my father deal with it because she knew that Florrie was seeking his attention.

Clifford never liked having a boss; he wanted to have his own business and so persuaded my father to get him a horse and cart so that he could go around selling fish. He knew a little about the business as he was working for Jack Francis, the fish merchant. My father also bought a trap so that we could go out on a Sunday. For a person with such a strong character, my mother had a surprising weakness – she was very nervous. We would go out in the trap, but she did not enjoy it, as she was afraid. The horse seemed to sense this as he would go as far as the cemetery and stop dead (no pun intended). My mother would get down and then he would trot on quite happily. We would only go a short distance and then turn around and pick my mother up on the way back. The horse was quite happy to take her home. However, there was no point in keeping the trap so my father sold it. We kept Tommy the horse, who was quite a character. His owner should never have sold him to us without warning us that he was temperamental.

My father's friend was a very good gardener and took part in flower shows, so my father offered him the use of his cart to take his entries to Merthyr. All went well until Tommy saw the hill at Abernant. Clifford pushed, tugged and coaxed, but Tommy would not move. At last, Clifford took off his dustcoat and wrapped it around Tommy's head – success at last! That is how they got to Merthyr.

Soon after that Clifford left home. A row flared up all over a spoonful of sugar. Clifford was shovelling it into his tea and my father had to tell him to go steady. That was it: he decided to leave. We thought he must have been planning to do so for some time because he went all the way to London. He came home one holiday and told Harry about the money he was earning. This impressed Harry no end as he was barely getting pocket money while being trained as a solicitor by a friend of my father.

Caroline and six-year-old Mabel

Caroline and Mabel, who was unhappy about wearing glasses for the first time

Caroline and Us

On the morning Clifford was due to return to London, we discovered that Harry had gone too, having left a lovely letter for my mother explaining why he had done it. She grieved for a long time, especially as he had given up such a promising future. My father sold the horse and cart and lost quite a lot of money on them, so they let the shop as a going concern to a middle-aged English couple by the name of Hounslow. They also rented some of our living quarters. Caroline and Mrs Hounslow shared the kitchen and got on very well, but then my mother would get on with anybody and she loved to chat.

My mother had now opened a fish and chip shop opposite the market, but she only opened it on market day and on Saturdays. It was very hard work as we had to prepare everything at home; the shop was too small. It was quite a busy shop, however, as Haggar's cinema was on the next corner and people would call in for fish and chips on the way home. We also had the football crowds as regular customers. On Saturday nights we had to clean the range and the shop before we left, so it meant that we were walking home at about two o'clock on Sunday morning, carrying all our pots and pans in a large tin bath. When we arrived home the local policeman would be waiting, because he knew my mother would be making a pot of tea.

The only contact that I remember making with Jimmy, my natural father, was in that shop on a Saturday. He would come in smelling of beer, and, speaking in Welsh, would demand a kiss. I never dared refuse although I found him revolting. My mother would not let me hurt anyone's feelings. I did have a slight reward; he would give me a couple of coppers, which I promptly spent on sweets in the market. These were mostly 'ladies ringers', a long pink-and-white-striped peppermint sweet which I bought on the boiled sweet stall.

My father was now working for Thomas and Evans, selling their 'pop' – four large bottles in a case, and delivered to your door for a shilling. There was a shilling to pay for the case, which was returned to you if you stopped buying the drink. I loved going with my father on his rounds as he also had a boy of my age helping him on a Saturday; it was great fun.

Life is full of coincidences. I went to a bar in Paddington with my boyfriend many years later and the barman was Benny, the boy on the cart. (You did not go into a bar on your own in those days, or if you did, you were considered to be 'on the make', as they genteelly put it.)

The Hounslows had been with us for about two years when they decided to buy their own shop a few blocks away on the other side of the road. We had a Pomeranian at that time, which my father said he had bought because she was the same colour as my hair. She had a splendid tail which used to fan out so we named her Fan. The word did not have a hidden meaning in those days. We also had gay parties – another adjective that did not have a double meaning back then. To get back to my story, Fan became very attached to the Hounslows. Whenever she went missing, we knew where she was and I was sent to fetch her from their shop. I think the peanuts they sold were also an attraction – she loved them. We used to give them to her in their shell and have fun watching her get the nuts out. We were amazed that she did not get run over as we lived at the side of a main road.

Hard Times

WE WERE now well into the depression and business was not as good. My mother decided to put the fish and chip range in our own shop as it would mean less work and save on the rent. People could not find the shillings to buy the pop from my father and since part of his wage packet was the commission he earned, he was getting very little money. It nearly broke my heart when he decided to go to London to work and I knew that it meant we would eventually go too. I missed my father very much but he used to take us out for a little treat in the summer. My mother would have a custard tart with ice cream, and my father and I would have ice cream in milk. In the winter it was a pork pie with plenty of sauce, and a cup of tea.

We could no longer afford to go on the charabanc outings as we used to do. If my father had been a drinking man we would never have been able to afford this. He was not at all bigoted about the drink; he just said that it did not agree with him, but if my uncles came to visit, he would go to the pub with them and stand his round. My mother had to manage the shop on her own, which meant she had to attend to the fires in the range as well as all the other jobs.

At last the dreaded news came: my father had found us a flat and we were to move to London. His cousin and family had a basement flat in Barons Court and his wife acted as housekeeper to the owner of the house, who was an English master in Colette Court School, which was the junior section of St Paul's School. This meant that if he employed my mother we would live rent free. My father's cousin had been lucky enough to have a flat in Lewis Buildings. A philanthropist had left money in his will to be used to build flats to let at a reasonable rent, and to get one of these the family had been well vetted to see if they were of good character. I was happy to be going to my father, but sad because I was leaving so much behind. My mother had always kept in touch with my family, and my niece and nephews were my friends. I had already lost young Caroline, as Sara-Jane and family had gone to America. I was closer to Florrie and my cousin Mary and her daughter Phyllis; if I ever wanted anything I would ask Florrie for it, and Mary used to make dresses for Phyllis and me. I remember my brother-in-law, Jared, putting me in an awkward situation one time; he asked me which of my sisters I liked best. When I did not reply, he said, 'None of the b—s ever give you anything!' Nevertheless, I was going to miss them.

I was going to have to leave my dog behind, but luckily Fan was going to a home where I knew she would be happy – the Hounslows were taking her. There was also a piece of furniture to which, for some reason, I was very attached. It was a beautiful sideboard which must have come from the house of gentry. It was very ornate with a mirror across the middle and beautiful carvings. The drawers were lined with baize, and there was a huge zinc-lined drawer for storing wine. My father must have bought it at an auction because he loved going to auctions. He had once brought home a guitar, although Clifford was the only one who could do anything with it, even though, with the exception of Harry, we had all had music lessons. The sideboard was too big to fit into a small flat so, to my sorrow, we had to leave it behind.

There was one thing which I was happy to be getting away from, and that was my Saturday job. My parents had turned our conservatory into a kitchen, complete with gas stove and I was a nervous wreck for days, waiting for the explosion which I was sure was going to happen. The floor had ridged tiles, as did the outside toilet, and it was my task on a Saturday to wash these floors. It used to take me ages as the water would get into the ridges and I had difficulty drying the floor. By the time I had finished, the water which had been hot was cold and miserable and I hated it.

My mother had to organise the move and sort out what was to be done with the house. She took it all in her stride; I believe she enjoyed a challenge and did not mind moving. She was unlike me in that I hate change. She had to leave me behind with Mary so that I could finish the term at school and I went to London in December 1929. The move was made easier because Mary allowed Phyllis to come with me. We were both thirteen years of age and we had a friendship which endured, with only one quarrel, until she died at the age of eighty-three. We were not a quarrelsome family; I never remember hearing of any bad feeling.

Our train arrived early in Paddington, so we sat on a bench to wait for my mother. We were approached by a policewoman who wanted to know all about us. She waited with us until my mother arrived; they seem to have been far more vigilant then. As it turned out, we were only a three-penny bus ride from our new home.

London

To say that I was less than impressed by our new home would be putting it mildly. It was certainly a comedown after what I had been accustomed to. We were quite near Barons Court Station, and the trains rumbled past our bedroom window. However, we soon became used to this. The cooking my mother had to do for Mr Down the schoolmaster was a little more sophisticated than she was used to, but she coped. We spent our first Christmas in London with my father's cousin John and his family. It was quite a happy one as he had two daughters a little older than Phyllis and me – it helped me to forget how homesick I was. In the New Year my mother took me to see the head of the grammar school to which I hoped to be transferred from Aberdare. She was quite elderly and did not inspire me with confidence. Her hair was in a knot on top of her head, with wisps hanging down over her face (sounds like it would be fashionable today), and her cardigan was halfway down her arms. She even asked my mother whether I could speak English. She finally decided to accept me when she was satisfied that the serge material of my gymslip was of a good enough quality; my mother and I had a good laugh about it on our long walk home.

Phyllis had gone home as it was time for her to go back to school after the Christmas holidays, and the time soon arrived for me to start school at the Munsler Road Secondary School. It was quite a long walk from where we lived and I could not afford the bus fare as it meant taking two buses. I also walked home at lunchtime as the school lunches were ten pence a day, which we also could not afford. I did not realise how short of money we were until I criticised my mother for not dressing as well as she used to in Aberdare – she told me that she could not afford to dress as well. When we lived in Aberdare, she had a friend in Penrhiwceiber who owned a boutique. When Mrs Davies went to the warehouses, if she saw anything which she thought would suit Florrie or my mother, she would buy it. My clothes, other than the dresses which Mary made for me, were made by a local dressmaker. We were so badly off when we first went to London that I had to go to school for a fortnight wearing wellington boots, regardless of the weather. I always felt quite embarrassed, but luckily none of the girls at school made any remarks.

I fitted in quite easily at school and was not treated any differently because I was Welsh. I especially enjoyed the drama lessons and was soon taking leading roles in school plays. During the celebrations for George V and Queen Mary, I had the honour of performing in what was then the County Hall, which was on the opposite side of the river to the Houses of Parliament. We were now also in contact with Clifford and Harry.

When we were running the shops, there were times my mother needed some help in the house: Doris was our first helper. She was only fifteen and a pretty blonde. The boys used to tease her and I became very friendly with her. Her family were quite poor; her father was unable to work as he was suffering from shell shock, caused by the war. My mother used to give her Florrie's old clothes. Florrie had looked very nice in them, but Doris would put a stitch here and a tuck there and she would look fabulous in them. Then we had Charlotte, a real Dolly Daydream. She was so slow that it was well into the afternoon before she finished her work. We came to the conclusion that she would rather be in our house than at home. The only way my mother could get her to hurry would be to tell her that there was a very good film on at Haggar's, and that it was starting early.

The last one was Ethel and she was a very capable girl. She was our neighbour, and we were friends of her family. We knew that Clifford liked her but did not realise how friendly they had been. Ethel had followed him to London as she had a sister living there; they were married soon after that and Harry lodged with them. Until just before she died, Ethel had thought that my mother was against the marriage because she did not think she was good enough for Clifford. The boot was actually on the other foot; my mother did not think Clifford was good enough for Ethel. She did not think he would be able to support her as he had not really settled down.

We had a great deal to thank my father's cousin for, as he told us that he had spoken to the superintendent of Lewis Buildings, and if my father went to see him, there was a possibility that we could have a flat. They were very comfortable flats with two bedrooms, a large living room with a serving hatch through to the kitchen. We had a separate bathroom and toilet, and a small balcony. There was only one drawback; we were now near Olympia which was a longer walk to the school than before. I considered it worth the effort to live somewhere that was more like our home though.

We settled quite happily in our new flat and were never short of company. Phyllis came to London to work as a children's nanny. Auntie Maggie's daughter, Blodwen, came to work for Lady Brunner, and Uncle Billy's daughter and her husband took a post as housekeepers. Florrie was very happy in Merthyr because she had become very friendly with a family who treated her like a daughter. Although the son of that family became her boyfriend, she wanted to come to London to be with her own family. She was taken on as a trainee nurse at the Western Hospital in Fulham; my mother also worked there in the kitchen. My father was working as a salesman, and whenever he contacted Welsh people he liked, he would invite them home. We had a close and lasting friendship with one couple who came from the Dowlais – they were Llew and Jenny Rhys. My father also met a woman he had known in Aberdare, and we became very friendly with her and her son. As we were only a threepenny ride from Paddington, lots of trippers from home would call to see us. As well as this, we had some who would spend a few days with us (no payment). This meant that I had to give up my bed and sleep on the sofa on which I could not get a proper night's sleep. It affected me so much that my form mistress asked me what was wrong – I looked like a death's head.

How my mother managed, I'll never know. She pulled the door of the food cupboard open one day and told me not to say a word as she had at last managed to build up a stock of food.

My mother always said that she hated Christmas as everything bad seemed to happen to her then, but that did not stop her from making sure that we all had a good time. We always had a crowd of visitors and we would play silly party games. I remember one Christmas in particular; we were all sitting there when suddenly Mrs

Browning, my father's friend from Aberdare, started to sing – it was diabolical. She may have had a good voice at one time but those days were long gone. Her son, Artie, discreetly left the room, while we all sat there with aching ribs through trying to suppress our laughter.

★

My father became ill and could only speak in a whisper; there was a problem with his larynx. As he was a salesman this meant that he was unable to work, and no work meant no pay at that time, so we had very little income. Fortunately, my mother was then working as a cleaner for Miss Myfanwy Jones who owned a large house in Avonmore Road – it was let out as separate bedsits.

Clifford and Ethel had a little daughter, Barbara, who used to stay with us sometimes. She made us laugh, because when my father spoke to her in a whisper, she replied in the same way. We were all very fond of her.

I needed a white overall for cookery lessons at school, and I was getting into serious trouble because I did not have one. My mother told me that she could not afford to buy me one that week as she was short of money. I accepted her answer, given the situation, but on the Saturday she could not resist buying a dress she had fancied for Barbara. I did not begrudge Barbara the dress, but I felt that my mother had not been fair with me. This was the only time that I ever felt that my mother had let me down. It is rather funny that although we were very hard up, we never felt poor – I believe that poverty is largely in the mind. In those days we did not worry about what other people had; there was not the bitter envy that there seems to be today.

David Eynon as a young man

My father, David, as I knew him

Harry had married his girlfriend, Flo. She was a typical Londoner and a charming person. They had broken off the relationship for a while. Harry was the intelligent and more serious one of the family and Flo was not his equal in this respect; this is why they parted. However, Flo was involved in a very serious road accident and that is when Harry went back to her; we were all pleased and they had a very happy marriage.

Jimmy had by now found his way to London and was in touch with the two boys. Clifford was more tolerant of him than Harry, but then Clifford had never had the dubious pleasure of living with him. He would go to Clifford when had run out of beer money and Clifford would give him a few shillings. I never saw him, nor did I ever want to; he had never been a father to me. I only had one father and that was David Eynon.

When I was sixteen and ready to sit for my Matric, as the exams were then called, my headmistress asked to speak to my parents. I was very uneasy in the week before they met her as I wondered what sort of trouble I was in. I need not have worried; she was concerned about my name. I had always used my father's name, but as I had not been legally adopted, I would have to use Jimmy's name, which was Dallimore, and she thought that this might cause me embarrassment. My father had been able to avoid this problem when I sat for my scholarship in Aberdare as he'd had a few words with the people in the education office. He now promptly set the wheels in motion to adopt me. I remember going to the court in Notting Hill where I was asked if I wanted to live with my parents. I wanted to laugh at the absurdity of the question; I had known no other parents since I was five months old.

My father did not stay in his work as a salesman for very long after his illness. He found out that Singer wanted a manager for their shop in Teddington and because of his good record, he was appointed. He was very clever at repairing sewing machines and made a hand machine for me built entirely out of the parts of old machines. I had started making my own clothes; it was either that or go without. I did not enjoy sewing and felt quite ill if I kept on sewing too long. There was another drawback: I had to sew for Florrie and my mother, although Florrie would offer to buy material for me as well as for her, if I would do the sewing. This was an opportunity too good to be missed.

Florrie was now nursing at the Fountain Mental Hospital in Tooting. Gwen and Megan Prowle had come from Aberdare to work there and had persuaded Florrie to join them. Because of the nature of the work, the wages and the free time were very much better than in a general hospital. Florrie and I used to go about a lot and our favourite night out was a visit to the 'Welsh Corner' at Marble Arch. We would walk there and back across Hyde Park, but we had to be home by ten o'clock or our father would be out looking for us. My mother, Florrie and I loved a shopping spree to Kensington High Street. We had no need to go up to town as we had C&A, Pontings, Barkers and Derry and Toms. The latter was just for window shopping as they were too expensive for us. I was always happy when Florrie bought herself new shoes because I knew that they would soon be given to me. She liked good shoes but she seemed to be unlucky – they were never as comfortable as they were in the shop and so they would come to me quite quickly. She was rather petite and had her clothes tailored, but I was not lucky enough to inherit these as I was rather lanky.

I had passed my exams with sufficient qualifications to go to teacher training college, but not enough for a scholarship, which was available in London at the time. My father decided that he had kept me for eighteen years and it was easier to keep me for another year than it was to find the college fees. I enjoyed that year very much as I had a great deal of free time which I used to spend practising to play the piano. This was essential as I was going to train as an infants' teacher. The next year I won my scholarship and was accepted at Avery Hill College in Eltham. Once again, my parents were requested to visit the headmistress.

Our friends, Llew and Jenny Rhys, had bought a new house in Worcester Park, Surrey, where there were new estates being built. My father was very interested as he had always owned his own house in Aberdare. After looking at several estates, he decided to buy a house on the same estate as Llew and Jenny. This was in 1935 and it cost £510 – the extra £10 was because he had a corner house. I told my headmistress about my change of address and that is why she asked to see my parents urgently. She advised them to keep a London address, otherwise I would lose my scholarship as the county of Surrey did not have them. Miss Jones came to our rescue. She had been the matron of a nursing home in Llanberis, and so they asked her to come back. My parents moved into her house to act as caretakers, and so we had a London address. They spent their weekends in Worcester Park, complete with the cat who travelled in a holdall.

Loss and Love

MY FATHER did not have the pleasure of his house for long, as he became very ill, and at the end of January 1936, my cousin Blodwen came to fetch me from college, as my father was dying in St George's Hospital, Hyde Park Corner. My mother decided that she would take him back to Aberdare to be buried, as she knew that is what he would wish. We were very fortunate in that we had a friend in Aberdare who owned coaches, and so he came up to fetch us.

I would have given up college in order to earn some money to help my mother but when I told Llew this, he said that if I did I would be letting my father down as he had set such store on one of his children becoming a teacher. He would have loved to have been a teacher himself and had even started training but had been obliged to give up when his father had suffered a stroke. So back I went, reluctantly, to college, but my heart was not in it. I was grieving so much for my father that I could not concentrate on my work and I could not sleep. They were very kind in my hostel, however, and made sure that I had a cup of hot milk at night to help me sleep. I had a dream one night: there were three men walking down a road in a wide beam of light. They were talking and laughing, and as they came nearer I could see that the middle one was my father. He said to me, 'I am quite happy, you know. Had I lived I would have been blind, and I would not have liked that.' That helped me to stop grieving.

It is said that a well-written tragedy always has episodes of light relief, and also that life and art mirror each other. We found this to be true when my father died. We stayed with Mary for a few days after the funeral, and my mother, Florrie and I went around visiting old friends. Everywhere we went we were promised the same things – a nice tin of salmon, with pears and cream to finish off. People were giving us the best they had, as these were luxuries at that time. We had so much salmon we were afraid we were going to grow fins. We visited some friends in Pontypridd and she told us, 'Now, you can choose. I have some cold lamb (it must have been a Monday), or—'

I did not give her time to say, 'A nice tin of salmon'. I jumped in quickly and said, 'Oh lamb, please!'

It was not particularly funny but we laughed about it all the way home to Mary's. It relieved the tension within us and we felt better for it.

My mother did not say much, but I knew she was missing my father – they used to do everything together. She loved the cinema and she and I would go in the afternoon when I was on holiday from school. There was a cinema in Hammersmith where we could get in for four pence and have a cup of tea as well. My father would only go to the cinema if there was a good comedy film, his favourite comedian being Harold Lloyd, so sometimes we had to go in the evening as well as the afternoon. My mother would tell me that she wished he would go on his own, but I know that in her heart she was pleased that he still enjoyed her company.

She lost a tremendous amount of weight after he died. She could not face living in the house on her own, so she put her furniture in storage and let the house. She was not happy in Miss Jones' flat either and luckily Miss

Jones was due back home. My mother took a bedsit in Talgarth Road, Barons Court. It was February and the fireplace was blocked up and there was no other means of heating in the room. The landlady pretended that there was something wrong with the chimney, but my mother insisted that she had to have a fire. In those days you had no need to have a coal delivery because you could buy brown paper bags full of coalite from garages and hardware stores. It was not as warm as coal, but it was a lot more convenient and much cleaner.

Once we had a fire going my mother was never short of company as the landlady enjoyed the warmth. All she had in her basement flat was an ordinary oil lamp in a bucket. The bucket was perforated and was lined with red tissue paper to give the illusion that it was warm. She was Belgian and very interesting to talk to.

The landlady insisted on making our bed herself and on one occasion she made us laugh. It so happened that Florrie and I were home at the same time as Mary was paying us a visit. Mary slept in the chair, and we three slept in the bed. The landlady came to make the bed as usual and she asked, 'How many hollows shall I punch this time? Four? First you come, then Mabel and Florrie, and then Mary-Jane come!' (My mother still called her Mary-Jane.) The landlady's name was Madam Lamer, and many years later we read in the newspaper that she had been murdered by one of her tenants.

Once more, my mother found herself a job. She worked for a Mrs Zenavov who had been a member of the Russian aristocracy. They had fled to England during the revolution in 1917. My mother used to bring special Russian cakes home. They were flat, white and tasted slightly of peppermint.

Talgarth Road was a rather expensive area so my mother could not afford to stay there more than a few weeks. She only had her ten shillings a week widow's pension and what she earned at Mrs Zenavov's. There was no profit from the house as that money paid for the mortgage and the agent. Somehow she managed to send me the occasional five-shilling postal order, however, which was spent mainly on art and craft materials. Luckily my fare home only cost two shillings for a return on the Greenline bus. I managed to save a few coppers from the one shilling and sixpence allowed us for lunch when we were out on school practice. At that time girls did not frequent public houses and there was no drug culture. Our idea of a good time was an ice cream sundae, a cup of tea and a cake, or a night at the cinema.

The room my mother moved to in Tregunter Road was far from satisfactory as she had nocturnal visitors – mice! Fortunately, she did not stay there long as she had already applied for a flat back at Lewis Buildings, and one became available quite soon.

By the time I had finished college in 1937, my mother had moved back into our own house in Worcester Park, as our tenants had bought a house in the next road. I signed on for supply teaching with Kingston and Epsom. The permanent post I had been offered was in Hull and we had no desire to move there. Once again, luck was on our side as I was given a long-term post just up the road from where we lived. In later years it was the school attended by my daughter.

Llew and Jenny Rhys introduced us to Olwen and Will-Ifor Evans, who were members of the Wimbledon Welsh Society; they took me along with them and I also became a member. It was only then that I really settled down in London; before that I would gladly have gone back to Aberdare. I also joined the dramatic society and played quite a few leading parts. My mother was busy getting the house and garden to her liking; she had no need to work since she had my salary coming in every month, out of which I received pocket money. That was the custom back then. Florrie had stopped contributing to the home when my father died. As she had resided where she was working she had never needed to hand over her salary, but she had always made a contribution.

★

In February 1938, I met Dave at a fancy dress party at the Welsh club. We soon started dating seriously, so when my mother and I went to Porthcawl on holiday in August we visited Dave's home in Ewenny, so that our mothers could meet each other. Neither of us had a father, as mine had died at the age of fifty-nine and so had his. Our mothers became good friends, as we had hoped they would. Not long after we returned home my mother told me that she had come to a decision. She was going to let the house, and Florrie and I could share a flat, which we did in Tooting. I think my mother, realising that Dave and I were thinking of marriage, felt that I should have more money for myself and not bear the cost of running the home. I think she was also getting restless as she was so accustomed to working and was not enjoying the idle life.

She found herself a live-in post as cook/housekeeper to a Mr Boothby, who lived in Dwyfor House, a luxury flat on the opposite end of Addison Bridge to Olympia. I believe he might have become Lord Boothby as one of his daughters was married to the son of Harmsworth, the newspaper tycoon – there was a connection between Lord Boothby and Harmsworth.

Mr Boothby soon moved from Dwyfor house, so my mother took a flat in Anselm Road, Walham Green. Things were beginning to get uneasy on the Continent and there was talk of war. I was now living in Kingston as Florrie was finding the flat too expensive so Dave's friends took me in as a boarder. We lived near to Kingston barracks and there was a lot of movement of military equipment there. It looked quite ominous.

War is Declared

THERE seemed to be troops of soldiers coming into London, which meant to us that war was imminent. Neither Dave nor I had a home in London so we decided to get married immediately so that when he was called up for military duty he would have a home to come back to. We went to Kingston Registry Office on 2 September 1939 and arranged for a special licence so that we could get married on 9 September. We did not think it would be right to bring Dave's mother to London when it was in such a state of upheaval. As we were not going to tell her that we were getting married, we decided it was only fair that my mother should not be told either. We just had my landlady and her sister as witnesses, and then we went to Bentall's Tudor Restaurant for lunch. Dave then sent his mother a telegram and we bought a piece of fruitcake and a bottle of sherry, which we took over to my mother to break the news. It was naturally a shock to them both as they were expecting us to marry the following June. I think my mother was secretly pleased because neither of us could afford to pay for a big wedding.

Dave and I now had the task of finding somewhere to live. It was left mainly to me as he worked away from home so often. I found just what we were looking for, and at a price we could afford, near to the Kingston Gate of Richmond Park. However, the landlord refused to let it to us because Dave was likely to be called up to the

*Caroline (wearing a dress made by Mabel)
and David with Llew in 1935*

Mabel and Caroline in Porthcawl in 1938

army. I thought it was disgusting and he would never have got away with doing that today. As it happened, Dave was not called up as he was in a reserved occupation; he worked on airfields for his firm as a bulldozer driver. It was quite hazardous as they often had to run for cover when the German planes flew low and strafed the airfield with bullets.

The bombing in our area was sporadic at first, but they were concentrating on London. My mother was a worry to us as she would insist on going home to her flat in Walham Green. She said she had to be there to look after her furniture; besides, she liked her work in the local pie factory. Putney was very badly bombed; some young people in a dance hall were killed one evening, and we were hoping that she had arrived home safely. We were never more thankful for the telephone as she was able to let us know that she was safe. We even found her a small flat in Kingston where she could put her furniture and come to us for her meals; we were not sure that she was feeding herself properly.

★

Our daughter, Lynda, was born in January 1943 and my mother stayed with me for three weeks to look after me. To be honest, I was not sorry when she went home as I was getting depressed doing nothing and it worried me to see my mother doing all the work as she was no longer a young woman. She was only about five foot tall but she was a bundle of energy and would not let anything defeat her. My mother's second cousin, Mary-Hannah, who I called Bopa, which was Welsh slang then for auntie, had taken one of the bedsits in the house we were in. She had brought her adopted daughter to London as she thought there were more opportunities for her than in a small village like Tycroes.

I had to go to Wales to help look after Dave's mother who was ill. I was away for a month, and I do not think it would have worried Dave had I stayed away for another month as he was being thoroughly spoiled between my mother and Bopa. My mother would come over from Walham Green several times a week to make sure that he had clean clothes and enough food, and she would also tidy the place. Bopa used to have chickens sent up from her home and there were always some for Dave.

Bopa's daughter, Nina, was a very attractive girl and the American soldiers must have thought she was too as she had several American boyfriends. The American and Canadian troops were both stationed in Kingston. The bombing of our area began to escalate and the night sky was always lit up by the searchlights from the barracks. We watched as they swept from side to side over the sky; sometimes a fighter would be caught in their beams. We knew which were ours by the sound of their engine. One night, we saw a dogfight above St Luke's Church, which was opposite our house. Eventually the German turned tail and fled with our fighter chasing him. Another night, a small plane went past our bedroom window and I remarked to Dave that some poor devil was in trouble as there were flames coming from the rear of the plane and a staccato of sound as if bullets were exploding. It turned out that it was not one of our planes but the very first V-1, or 'buzz bomb' as we came to call them. It exploded in a wood yard on the other side of the Thames.

At first we sheltered in the cellar during bombings, but then we had an Anderson shelter in our living room.

It was like a huge metal table, under which we slept when the bombing was bad. We had plenty of room for it. The man who had refused us his flat had really done us a good turn, as what we ended up with was very much better. We lived in the rooms which were once occupied by the owner of the house and his family; the rest of the house was let as bedsits. We had two small bedrooms, privately situated along a corridor off the main landing and a very large lounge which held our dining-room suite, a three-piece suite and a piano – and we still had room to dance! Because it was a corner house, we had two large bay windows which were a bit of a problem because they had to be blacked out at night. Otherwise we would hear the warden shout, 'Put that r—dy light out!'

We also had a very large kitchen, a scullery, a walk-in pantry, an outside toilet, and a very big backyard and all for seventeen shillings and sixpence a week. All I had to do in return was keep the bathroom, hall and stairs clean. There were five bedsits in all and my mother said that she could not understand why I did not socialise more with the other tenants; but I had been warned by what had happened to her. When she was looking after Miss Jones' house, she had become so friendly with the tenants that she complained to me that she never had a minute to herself. I was not unfriendly and, in fact, had a good friend in the bedsit on the ground floor. We spent a lot of time together as her husband was in the forces and Dave had to go away so much. We respected each other's privacy; when Dave was home she kept away and I did the same when her husband was home.

We became very familiar with the number six as we lay under the shelter during the bombing raids. The

Florrie and Tom in Switzerland

Dave, Mabel, Bryn and Florrie, 1939

Germans dropped their bombs in 'sticks' of six, so that when we had heard the sixth explosion we knew that we had once again been spared. We now had a different sound to listen for which in some ways was not as frightening as the bombing raids. We were in the flight path of the V-1s and Bopa was really fascinated by them; she would sit at her window and watch them go by. They gave us fair warning when they were going to strike as their engines would cut out. There was increased activity from the barracks as the anti-aircraft guns were going day and night. My mother and Bopa persuaded me to take the baby away from London. Dave was working on an airfield in Stoke-on-Trent so I went to Birmingham of all places, so that he was able to visit us on some weekends.

Florrie had married Tom in December 1939 and in spite of them having had a long courtship, he had never been introduced to our father. This had quite upset him and he had based his judgement of Tom on what other people had told him. He had thus had a poor opinion of him, but he had been quite wrong, as Tom was a very decent man. Florrie would entertain him at home when she knew that we would all be out. She was the same with Tom as she had been with us. Mary and Ted were now living in Birmingham, and when Tom was sent there to work, they stayed with Mary for a while until they found accommodation. Florrie would be happy, talking and laughing all day until Tom came home, then she would be all tearful and complain to him about something or other. She told people that Tom would not let her do this or buy that, which was not true. We had a saying in our family, 'Do you want it, gel? Then have it!' because that is what Tom used to say to Florrie. It was such a pity that Florrie had this fault, which she just could not help, as, like her father, she was a loving and generous person. In any case, she managed all the money and did so very well, as they were able to buy their own house; after the war they went abroad on holiday every year, which few people were able to do at that time.

I decided that I would stay with Mary; as Florrie had no children, she had to work for the war effort. I reasoned that if I stayed with Florrie I would have to burn her coal ration during the day because of the baby, whereas Mary was home all day so she had to have a fire going anyway. Florrie only lived around the corner so I would spend every evening with her, and she appreciated why I made this choice.

My mother had moved from her flat in Anselm Road, which was rather big for one person, to a smaller flat off the Northend Road. She was not there long before she was bombed out – it was not a direct hit, but the flat was uninhabitable. Once more we tried to get her to move to Kingston, but with no more luck than before; she took a flat near to Lyon's Cadby Hall. She was now working as a messenger at the Admiralty in Whitehall but half her life was spent sheltering in the tube stations with hundreds of others. She was bombed out once again and I begged her to come and look after the baby while I went back to teach, and I said that we would share my salary. Lynda slept for a few hours in the afternoon so it would have been very easy for my mother to look after her. She had made up her mind, however, to put her furniture in storage and take a post as house mother in the children's home in Church Village, South Wales. Florrie and I were very worried about this as we doubted, after all she had been through, that she would be physically strong enough.

Such was my relationship with Florrie and Mary that I had not asked whether we would be welcome in their homes; we just turned up. Mary treated me like a daughter, and Florrie was my sister. I had rather a traumatic time at Mary's. To start off with, she decided to have some renovations done to her house; the bay window had a wooden base which was deteriorating so she decided to have a brick base built instead. Also, the surround of her fireplace was just painted plaster, and she wanted to have it tiled. The builder came along to do it, but instead of finishing one job at a time he removed the plaster and the wooden bay at the same time. He kept going away for hours on end with some excuse or other and then he would come back smelling of drink. The work seemed to be taking for ever. Mary spoke to him about it and he went off in a huff and never came back.

She was in a real mess, and in the middle of it she received a telegram from the war office to say that her son had been killed in India. Ted managed to get someone to finish the work so that was no problem, but Mary had turned stubborn. She was refusing to cook for her boarders; as her son was dead she saw no reason why she should look after other people's sons. Fortunately, the students had gone home so she only had two boarders left. Ted and I managed to cope. There was not much that Phyllis could do as she was married and living in Coventry; she had a four-year-old son and another one on the way.

Eventually we managed to persuade Mary to go to Aberdare for a break and life became a lot easier, although Ted took to his bed with lumbago. She was much more like her old self when she returned after three weeks. Dave had now been sent back to Surrey to work so I decided to go back home.

We had no sooner returned home than something far worse was sent to attack us – the V-2 flying bomb. It was really vicious and caused far more damage than a normal bomb. It gave us no warning; there was just an enormous explosion and you knew that it had arrived. The anti-aircraft guns were powerless against them as they had no target to aim for. It was only the bravery of our airmen – seeking out and bombing the point of departure of the V-2s – that saved us then.

Health Worries

MY MOTHER came home to us in a sorry state; what Florrie and I had expected had happened. My mother had suffered a breakdown and could not continue to work at the children's home. She had never been a fat woman but she had always been nicely rounded; now she was just a bag of bones and her skin was hanging in folds. She would complain of her stomach, but the doctor could find nothing wrong with it. He often supplied her with medicine, but I think it was just a placebo. She was not chewing her food properly and was vomiting it back in lumps. He was very patient with her and told me she was suffering from melancholia, and that the best thing for her would be for her to go to work. I understood his reasoning – he thought she needed the stimulation – but it was physically impossible as she just didn't have the strength. She then complained her head ached, so he sent her for an X-ray, but once again there was nothing to be seen. It was not surprising if she had headaches, as she would sit so close to the fire with her head on her lap that you could smell the grease drying out of her hair.

She used to enjoy taking Lynda out in the pram until Dave's mother asked her whether she was nervous. That was it; she decided that she could not walk, but it was all in the mind. She would sit by the fire looking quite unkempt and her clothes would be stained by the medicine she spilled on them; but then she would arrive some mornings looking spick and span in her 'West of England tweed costume'. We knew, when she was dressed that way, that one of two things was going to happen: she was either going to Kensington to visit her friend, Miss Jones, or she had a date with the man friend she had acquired when she was in the Admiralty. She would get cross if we asked her where she was going and always said she was only going for a little walk. I did not worry about her, though, as she had so much willpower that I knew she would come to no harm. The doctor was still attending to her, and he very kindly recommended that she be sent to a convalescent home on the east coast for three weeks. He was only able to do this because she had attended hospital for an X-ray – only people who had been in hospital were supposed to go. Bopa took her there on a Monday as she was too weak to go on her own, but on the following Friday, our back door opened and there was my mother. She had struggled home on her own as she said that she had not gone down there to wash dishes and make beds and, furthermore, they had said they had seen her running up the road, which was a lie. So that was that!

My mother's health now began to deteriorate both mentally and physically, and she spent most of her time in bed. This was very worrying as she shared a very small bedroom with Lynda and she refused to have the blackout curtains drawn back during the day, making the room very stuffy and unhealthy. There was also an element of danger as we could not rely on my mother; one minute she could not walk and the next she would be walking without difficulty. We were afraid that she might fall down the stairs and hurt herself, so as a temporary measure we put her bed in the lounge. We knew we would have to move it into the living room for the winter as the lounge was so big, and with the two bay windows it would be difficult to keep it warm enough for her.

Clifford and Ethel were visiting us one day and Ethel asked me about the lump on my neck. I had no idea that I had a lump so she made me promise to go to the doctor, who said that I had an overactive thyroid and should not be looking after my mother. I let Florrie know and she and Tom came down to fetch her so that I could have a break. While my mother was with Florrie she became incontinent. Florrie could not cope with this as she was having to work because of the war, besides which my mother needed treatment. She was taken into hospital where they sedated her for over three months; she later accused us of not having visited her because she was unaware that we had been there.

The tenants in our house in Worcester Park were there on a lease that had run out. I thought that if I could get the house back for her it would help to cheer her up. The tenants refused to move, and they were also in arrears with the rent so I took them to court. They made the mistake of telling lies. They said that they had two young children, when I knew for a fact that both their daughters had left school and one was engaged to a Canadian soldier.

I can hear the judge now saying, 'Pay your rent, woman, and be out by the fifteenth of August.' We moved in during the VJ celebrations and I sorted out my mother's furniture, which had been in store in Aberdare. I made one of the bedrooms into a bedsit for her if she ever felt she wanted a break from us. The remainder of the furniture went to Florrie as she had some empty rooms in her house. I had to clean the furniture that came to me, as there was jam, rice and soot all over it from the bombing of my mother's flat. When everything was ready for her, my mother came home and she was almost her normal self.

But then my mother became even more difficult to live with; she was no longer her old easy-going self. She used to be very fond of Dave, yet now he could do nothing right as far as she was concerned. I used to dread the window cleaner coming as she would bang on the window and tell him he was not doing his work properly. I had to have a little word with him and he was very understanding. We also had a traffic island opposite our house and if any children dared to go on it she would shout at them. She loved going to Aberdare on holiday, but I was not as happy about it as she would come home absolutely worn out. She could not accept that she was now physically incapable of behaving as she used to – she had been so active in her younger years.

Hints kept coming my way that I should return to teaching, which I did not wish to do until Lynda started school. Finally, to pacify my mother, I took a part-time post in a private school in Surbiton, and later I did part-time teaching in a school five minutes' walk from home.

Matters did not improve at home; the minute I opened the front door I would either have complaints from my mother about Lynda or vice versa. Mercifully, Lynda started school and I started working full-time. My mother went on holiday to Porthcawl with her friend, Esther-Ann, from Aberdare. I thought the sea air would be beneficial and that she would come home feeling better; on the contrary, she came home in poorer health than ever and took to her bed once more. I was now

Caroline and Llew (seated) and Jenny (behind her), 1939

Caroline with Esther-Ann (second left) in Porthcawl, 1946

between the devil and the deep sea as I did not know whether to give up my job or not. She was so keen that I should be teaching and she had periods when she was practically normal, so I was afraid that if she found out that I had given up my job because of her, it would be enough to tip her over the edge again.

When my mother was not working she was a late riser, and loved her bed in the morning. My father used to tease her and say in Welsh, *'Os carad di'r bedd fel carad di'r gweli, ti fydd yr olaf yn adgofodi,'* which meant, 'If you love your grave as you love your bed, you'll be the last in the resurrection.' So I had a word with the headmistress, who was very understanding and allowed me to teach mornings only as I considered my mother to be quite safe in her bed in the mornings.

My mother was now a lot easier to live with as she was not mentally fit, though it was harder work for me physically, as she was more helpless, and I had to give up my membership of the dramatic society and my job as secretary of the Wimbledon Welsh Society. As my mother's bedroom was next door to the bathroom, and opposite the head of the stairs, I put a very heavy chair across the stairs just in case she decided to go to the bathroom. If she had stumbled the chair would have prevented her from falling, but I came home one day to find that she had moved the chair. We decided then that we could not trust her upstairs, as one minute she was apparently helpless and the next she would be coming down the stairs. Visitors would call to see her and they would ask me how she was. I would tell them that she was too weak to hold a cup of tea. They would go in to see her and she would sit up and hold her cup of tea as steady as a rock. Fortunately we saw the funny side of it. If we had not laughed we would have cried to see her like this.

We thought she would be safer with her bed downstairs in the dining room and I used to take her into the lounge for a few hours in the afternoon. She did not like staying up for too long a period and would say, 'I think I would like to go home now,' and so I would take her back to her bed. I thought sometimes that it would be a blessing if she died because she was not really living. Then I was ashamed of myself for thinking this as she seemed quite happy in her own little world into which she had retreated. She went into Epsom Hospital for a short while in the hope that they could do for her what they had succeeded in doing in Birmingham, but she was beyond help.

It was a difficult time for me, as I was torn between doing my duty to my mother and doing it towards Dave and Lynda. However, I was very lucky in that we had a good neighbour who would keep an eye on my mother for a few hours on a Saturday so that we could take Lynda to the cinema. I also had a good husband who never complained about my mother, nor did he resent her living with us.

One thing happened that cheered me up. My sister Nellie, who was now widowed, went on holiday to see Sara-Jane in America, and she brought me back a present. It was only the second present that I had ever had from my sister. May had sent me a dress for Lynda when she was born. I appreciated that very much as we had to surrender clothing coupons at that time if we wanted to buy clothes.

Friends told us about a very good nursing home that would be prepared to take my mother for a few weeks. She was there for three weeks and was quite happy; they said that she had been very good and they would welcome her at any time. This allowed us to have three carefree weeks when we were able to visit Dave's mother who was not in the best of health either. The knowledge that this option was open to us made a great difference to the way I felt, and as I was still working part-time we were able to afford it. Unfortunately, we never did do it again as my mother soon became worse and was bedridden. After a while, she had lost what little weight she had managed to put on and, since I had no real experience of nursing, it worried me that I was hurting her when I moved her in order to wash her and change her position to prevent bedsores. My fingers felt so hard on her tender body. I mentioned this to the doctor and he suggested putting her in hospital for a while.

While we were waiting for the ambulance to come for

my mother, I took her a cup of tea; but I found that she was in a deep sleep from which she never woke. She had suffered a cerebral haemorrhage in her sleep. I was grateful for the peaceful way in which she died and shed very few tears, as I had done my crying for my mother long before this. She was sixty-five years of age, and they said she was suffering from senile decay but to my way of thinking she was as much a casualty of the war as any soldier.

When the ambulance arrived they got in touch with the police, as it was regarded as a sudden death. Two police cars came screaming up to our house; why they needed two I will never know. Rumours were flying around our road that my mother had gassed herself – whoever started that rumour had a vivid imagination. They said that we could not make funeral arrangements as there would probably have to be a post-mortem, the death having been so sudden. We could not contact our doctor because he was away, but fortunately he returned on the Monday and reassured the police that the death was not unexpected as she had been his patient for four years. We had buried my father with Florrie's mother, so we took Caroline home and buried her with Henry-John.

The graves are sadly neglected because I am not a grave tender, but then there is nothing in them that has any meaning for me. I have my memories, and what remains of my parents is in my head and in my heart.

★

PS I did receive a letter from America from my uncle Walter, but not one of condolence as you might have expected. He was demanding a share of my mother's estate! But that's another story.

Looking Back

1.

This is a copy of a letter Hannah wrote to my eldest brother, Thomas-George, when he was in the army in what was then Mesopotamia. I still have the letter. She died in August 1916.

> 72 Monk Street,
> Aberdare.
>
> July 21st 1916

Dear son,

I now take the pleasure of writing to you these few lines hoping to find you well, as we are now at present. I received your letter alright but sorry to hear it is so warm there, we do grumble it is warm here so I don't know how you will put up with it, but take care of yourself and have everything you do want.

I am sending you five shillings as you said. I only wish I could send you something but let me know what you think I had better send you. I would send you more money but I want to know if you had the five shillings safe.

I had a letter from T Mendham on Saturday. It was last week he came out of hospital since he went back after his leave. I have had several letters from him asking have I heard from you. I sent him three shillings as his pay was stopped.

Dear son, I don't think I've got much news this time but I want you to cheer up and take care of yourself so we do all send our kind love to you.

From your loving mother.

xxxxxxxxxxxxxxxxx
xxxxxxxxxxxxxxxxx

2.

This is of interest in view of Caroline's unhappy experience:

Susie John's psychic helpline

25 November 2002

Q. Half asleep on the living-room sofa, I looked up to see a black cartoon-like figure of a dog creeping along the coving. It stopped, looked at me, then walked to the corner of the ceiling and disappeared into the wall. What was it?

A. It is possible that what you saw had nothing to do with you and everything to do with the house or someone who lived there. Dogs are usually a good omen, but this one is furtive, distrusting and lost. Black here relates to funerals and loss.

3.

In Praise of a Welsh Mountain

When travelling oft through Surrey's hills and dales,
Nostalgia filled me for the land of Wales,
For mountains full of character and scope;
A craggy challenge, not some gentle slope.

But not for me Garmarthen's mountains who,
Black by name and black by nature too,
Nor lofty Snowden wreathed in misty smiles,
Who careless climbers to their doom beguiles.

But the soft-bosomed mountain of my native place,
Where are no seams of coal to mar her face.
Four grassy rounded 'tumps' against the sky;
This was my goal, this paradise so high.

It was forbidden me in my youth to roam
All on my own, so very far from home,
For fear some lustful male perchance I'd meet,
Who'd rob me of my innocence so sweet.

Blind obedience never was my way.
What need of friend to curb imagination's sway?
Up there, unfettered by the rein of sense,
My span was endless and my power immense.

Oh joy! When having reached the top
To watch the bus lurch on from stop to stop,
To watch its journey up the mountainside;
When limbs are young, what joy is there to ride?

To see the rifts where feckless sheep may slip,
Or sightless lovers, wandering lip to lip,
May fall unduly, jolt themselves to earth,
And find in this some lovers' cause for mirth.

Then I would seek the luscious berries blue,
Which shyly hid from wind, from me and you.
And having found, I would myself regale,
Forgetting that my lips would tell a tale.

The sun descending from its perch would then
Tell me I was no eagle, but a wren;
And I must to my lowly state return,
But for this boundless vista still I yearn.

Ah! Would I find that now my youth has fled,
Imagination's sterile, cold and dead?
Or would the magic of my mountain still
My mind with long-forgotten fancies fill?

One day without a doubt I'll know;
Back to my mountain all alone I'll go,
Perchance to capture some of childhood's fun,
Perchance to rest there when my day is done.

M E Davies
2007

Printed in the United Kingdom
by Lightning Source UK Ltd.
123258UK00001B/147/A